SURVIVAL
IS EASY

JUST DON'T DIE

Thomas Woodsman

SURVIVAL IS EASY. JUST DON'T DIE

When disaster strikes, will you be ready?

Now is a great time to start—or continue—to plan, collect and organize what you need to survive in case of an emergency and many outdoor gear items you may already own can be quite useful in such instances.

To begin with we are going to discusses the 4 basic concepts of emergency and survival preparedness:

Storage and retrieval of supplies

Survival food and gear

Copies of important documents

Maintenance of your supplies

Storage and Retrieval of Supplies

Natural or human-made disasters can occur with little to no warning. So it's important to keep everything you need in one place, protected from the elements and easily accessed. Retrieving your supplies should be as easy as grabbing a bin, backpack or other container—a 1-step process that's crucial when every second counts.

Storage tips: Items you should have readily available at a moment's notice.

Use plastic bins or similar containers, or use a backpack or duffel bag wrapped in a clean garbage bag.
Store the container in your basement, outside in a storage shed, in your garage or even buried in your backyard.
Make sure everyone in your household knows where and how to retrieve it.

Hand-crank radio

Survival Food and Gear

FEMA, the Federal Emergency Management Agency, offers a detailed website full of useful information: www.ready.gov.

Their website recommends that you should include the following items in a basic emergency kit:

Water, 1 gallon of water per person per day for at least 3 days, for drinking and sanitation

Food, at least a 3-day supply of nonperishable food

Battery-powered or hand-crank radio and a NOAA weather radio with tone alert and extra batteries

Flashlight and extra batteries

First-aid kit (see below for details)

Whistle to signal for help

Dust mask to help filter contaminated air and plastic sheeting and duct tape to shelter-in-place

Moist towelettes, garbage bags and plastic ties for personal sanitation

Wrench or pliers to turn off utilities

Manual can opener for food

Local maps

Cellphone with charger, inverter or solar charger

Next, consider adding the following:

Prescription medications and glasses

Infant formula and diapers

Pet food and extra water for your pet

Cash or traveler's checks and change

Emergency reference material such as a first-aid book or free information from the (see the FEMA website's publications page)

Sleeping bag or warm blanket for each person; add more bedding for cold-weather climates

Complete change of clothing including a long-sleeved shirt, long pants and sturdy shoes; more clothing if you live in a cold-weather climate

Household chlorine bleach and medicine dropper*

Fire extinguisher

Matches in a waterproof container

Feminine supplies and personal hygiene items

Mess kits, paper cups, plates, paper towels and plastic utensils

Paper and pencil (a pen might not work in colder temperatures. A pencil always will.

Books, games, puzzles or other activities for children

* When diluted—9 parts water to 1 part bleach—bleach can be used as a disinfectant. Or in an emergency, you can use it to treat water by using 16 drops of regular household liquid bleach per gallon of water. Do not use bleaches that are scented, color safe or have added cleaners.

First-aid kit

A first-aid kit is a great resource to have handy at home, in the car and at work. The following first-aid items should be stored in an elements-proof container, or in a small backpack/pouch if stored under your desk or in a car.

Two pairs of latex or other sterile gloves if you are allergic to latex

Sterile dressings to stop bleeding

Cleansing agent/soap and antibiotic towelettes

Antibiotic ointment

Burn ointment

Adhesive bandages in a variety of sizes

Eye wash solution to flush the eyes or as general decontaminant

Thermometer

Prescription medications you take every day such as insulin, heart medicine and asthma inhalers; periodically rotate medicines to account for expiration dates

Prescribed medical supplies such as glucose and blood pressure monitoring equipment and supplies

Nonprescription drugs:

Aspirin or non-aspirin pain reliever

Anti-diarrhea medication

Antacid

Laxative

Other first-aid supplies:

Scissors

Tweezers

Tube of petroleum jelly or other lubricant

Copies of Important Documents

Stash your important family documents such as copies of insurance policies, identification and bank account records in a waterproof, portable container.

Tip: A sealable plastic bag tucked into a wide-mouth water bottle works great. Your important documents are protected and—voila!—you've secured an extra water vessel as well.

Maintaining Your Supplies

Every 6 months, check your food and emergency supplies. Refresh your water supply, consume and/or replace foods that will expire within the next 6 months, dispose of expired or damaged food, and add any items that may be needed. An addition to the household or changing medical needs may require different or additional supplies. Refer to the following list as you survey your stash:

Keep canned food in a cool, dry place.

Store boxed food in tightly closed plastic or metal containers to protect from pests and to extend the shelf life.

Throw out any canned good that becomes swollen, dented or corroded.

Use foods before they go bad and replace them with fresh supplies.
Place new items at the back of the storage area and older ones in the front.

Change stored food and water supplies every 6 months; be sure to write the date you store it on all containers.

Rethink your needs every year and update your kit as your family's needs change.

With just a little time, effort and money, you can be prepared with the supplies you and your loved ones need to survive when no other support or assistance is available. It is a wise and potentially life-saving investment.

Start today.

We have only just begun to get you up to speed on your survival skills. There is much more we need to cover so lets just keep going.

It can be pretty scary to live in a world with no light. The trouble is there might come a time when available light is at a premium such as when the power grid suddenly, and without warning, goes off line. Weather can cause this as well as many other "natural" circumstances. There could also be another cause for the outage and it could be one that we don't want to consider but in today's world of upheaval and threat of terrorists activities we have no option but to consider it as one reason for a possible power outage. Regardless of what happens you need to be prepared to have a light source that is dependable and constant without having to rely on an outside source of power to create it. So now we'll discuss batteries in depth and learn how to keep the lights on even when all around us has gone dark.

Battery Recommendations

Among rechargeables, Nickel Metal Hydride (NiMH) are tops: They offer long-term value for powering GPS receivers, headlamps and bike lights. They're also a good choice for small household items used frequently or continuously (toys, for instance) and "high-drain" devices such as digital cameras.

The upside of standard NiMH batteries:

They typically can be recharged and reused 150 to 500+ times. One set could do the work of hundreds and hundreds of single-use ("disposable") batteries. Nearly 3 billion single-use batteries, mainly alkaline batteries, are sold in the U.S. each year. The majority wind up in landfills. Ouch.

They outperform single-use batteries in "high-drain" devices such as digital cameras and GPS receivers. Early in their life cycle, NiMH batteries discharge energy more steadily (and thus longer) than single-use batteries. In a camera (which involves repeated power bursts), alkaline batteries start strong but fade quickly. In GPS units, alkalines generally perform well.

Downside:

They require fairly regular maintenance. NiMH batteries lose power when sitting idle, 1% or more per day. To keep them operating near their peak, standard NiMH batteries need to be recharged (and preferably used) every 1 to 2 months.

They grow less predictable as they age. Late in their life cycle, NiMH batteries hold charges for shorter periods. Tip: If you own many NiMH batteries, avoid mixing older and newer cells—keep them grouped.

Precharged NiMHs are the best rechargeables now available. These are also called "hybrid," "ready-to-use" or "low self-discharge" batteries.

Upside of precharged NiMH batteries:

Ready for action. They can go straight into a device. No initial charging needed.

Lower "self-discharge" rate than standard NiMH batteries. All batteries experience "self-discharge"—a loss of stored power when a battery is not in use. Standard NiMH batteries may lose up to 40% of their stored energy in a month and be fully empty in as little as 2 months. Precharged NiMHs minimize that loss, surrendering only 10% to 25% of their stored power over 6 months. They can serve as backup batteries for trips lasting up to a few months.

Downside:

Some maintenance is still required. If left idle, recharging is suggested every 6 to 9 months.

Slightly less energy capacity than standard NiMH batteries. During periods of continuous or intense activity in a short time frame (shooting photos at a wedding, for instance), standard NiHM batteries will probably outlast precharged NiMHs due to their modest advantage in energy capacity.

Single-use batteries make excellent backup batteries: They store well for years, are always ready for action and offer high energy capacity. Pricey lithium batteries are superb performers (especially in cold weather), but check your gizmo's instructions first before using them. Lithium batteries (at 3 volts per cell) can overpower some devices (headlamps in particular) and fry their circuitry. Alkaline batteries, meanwhile, are tried-and-true workhorses suitable for any device. In a GPS unit, for instance, they typically deliver about 2 days' worth of continual service. Their chief downsides: 1) rapid depletion when used in a digital camera and 2) their unending cycle of use-discard-replace.

No ideal battery exists: As the charging cycles add up, rechargeable batteries hold charges for progressively shorter stretches. No rechargeable battery lasts forever, though they can usually be counted on for years. Single-use batteries, meanwhile, are predictable and convenient, but over the long long-term are more expensive due to the endless need to replace them. Plus, each year billions wind up in landfills because many people aren't aware they can be recycled or don't make the effort to do so.

Battery performance is not predictable: Many factors—the type of device being powered; the frequency or strength of a power drain; the temperature; battery age—make it difficult to forecast how consistently a battery will perform. Keep in mind that your results may vary.

Batteries are evolving: Just like the microelectronic devices they power, today's mass-selling batteries will become tomorrow's dinosaurs. On the horizon: fuel cell batteries, thin-film polymers and batteries modified by nanotechnology.

Solar chargers are worth considering: For extended stays in remote corners of the planet, these ever-improving energy collectors can supply a moderate amount of power to your devices each day.

Now for a little Battery 101:
Battery Basics

Batteries are portable storehouses of energy. When activated, they furnish a flow (or discharge) of electric current. They date back to 1800 when Italian physicist Alessandro Volta invented the "voltaic pile"—a stack of blotting papers saturated by a briny stew of silver and zinc. In 1896 the National Carbon Company (which became Eveready, then Energizer) is credited for introducing the first battery marketed for consumer use: the 1.5-volt Columbia dry cell. In those days it measured 6 inches long.

Modern microelectronic devices such as headlamps and GPS receivers are powered by dry cell batteries such as the cylindrical AA batteries we all know. They are available in single-use or rechargeable models. In technical battery jargon, single-use batteries are known as "primary" batteries. Rechargeables are "secondary" models.

A dry cell battery has positive and negative terminals. Internal layers (electrodes) include a cathode (which transports a positive charge) and an anode (to carry a negative charge). They are divided by some type of barrier called a "separator." (Technical footnote: With rechargeable batteries, the cathode and anode carry reverse charges during recharging.)

Alkaline AA battery

In single-use alkaline batteries, the cathode is usually powdered manganese dioxide (sometimes mixed with graphite). The anode is zinc. Nickel, along with various alloys, is the dominant component of most cylindrical rechargeable batteries.

All batteries contain some type of electrolyte—a substance that conducts electricity (a flow of electrons) between a battery's terminals. Motor vehicles use large "wet cell" batteries where the electrolytes are liquid. In dry cell batteries, the electrolyte is more of an aqueous paste or gel.

When a battery is activated, the electrolyte, cathode and anode interact and a chemical reaction (basically oxidation) occurs. Ions (positively charged) and electrons (negatively charged) flow through the electrolyte, exit via the negative terminal and enable a device such as a headlamp (the "load") to function.

Lithium AA battery

Over time, a battery's internal chemicals begin to degrade and interaction diminishes. Eventually they can no longer retain a charge. In this depleted state, the battery is "dead."

The mix of chemicals in dry cells aims to provide some combination of the four holy grails of the elusive "ideal" battery—long life, high performance, reasonable cost and low environmental impact. A frustrating fact of battery life is that advancements in battery technology have not come close to keeping pace with the rapid rate of progress (and increasing power demands) in microelectronics.

Until the perfect battery arrives, here's a look at the portable power options now available to you:

Single-use Batteries

Alkaline

The most commonly used battery of all contains an alkaline electrolyte, usually potassium hydroxide.

Nominal voltage (the force that "pushes" electrons through a battery): 1.5 (though it gradually declines to less than 1 volt as battery discharges its energy).

Estimated shelf life (at 68°F/20°C): 5-7 years.

Best use: "Low-drain" devices such as LED headlamps, LED flashlights, toys, remote control devices, clocks and radios, even moderate-drain items such as lights using incandescent bulbs. Can be used in high-drain devices (digital cameras, for instance), though life expectancy will be sharply reduced. Why? Even though alkalines have high initial energy capacity, high-drain devices exert such a substantial draw that energy swiftly gets slurped out. As mentioned earlier, in a GPS receiver they typically deliver 2 days of continual use, or many days of periodic use.

Pros:

Moderately priced.
Widely available.
Estimated to provide about 300% more energy capacity than zinc chloride (so-called "heavy duty") or antiquated zinc carbon ("general purpose") batteries.

Cons:

Perpetual cycle of use-disposal-replacement. Most end up in landfills.

Note: Some rechargeable alkaline batteries exist, but they typically can accept only a few charges. They are widely viewed as a failed technology. Lithium

Lithium, an exceptionally light metal, gives lithium batteries the highest energy density of any battery cell. Thus they can store more energy than alkaline batteries or any single-use battery of a comparable size.

USE WITH CAUTION: Their higher voltage capacity makes lithium batteries too powerful for some devices and may damage circuitry. Read manufacturer instructions for battery recommendations for individual products.

Nominal voltage: 3 (though it gradually declines as battery discharges).

Estimated shelf life (68°F/20°C): 10-15 years.

Best use: "High-drain" devices (digital cameras) and most (but not all) lower-drain microelectronic devices. They are too powerful, for example, for some headlamps.

Pros:

Longest life (by far) in single-use category; in a digital camera, lithium batteries hypothetically may produce 100-200+ flash photos; alkaline batteries, 20-40+.

Superior functionality in cold weather (particularly subzero temperatures) and hot conditions.

Estimated to provide about 300% more energy capacity than zinc chloride (so-called "heavy duty") or antiquated zinc carbon ("general purpose") batteries.

Longer shelf life.

Lowest weight.

Cons:

More expensive.

WARNING: Higher voltage may damage some devices. Read manufacturer instructions that accompany each device to determine if they can handle lithium batteries.

Note: What is the difference between lithium and lithium-ion batteries? Lithium batteries cannot be recharged. Lithium-ion batteries can.

Heavy Duty or General Purpose

These are the ancestors of alkaline batteries. The electrolytes used are zinc chloride (heavy duty) or zinc carbon (general purpose).

Nominal voltage: 1.5 (gradually declines to less than 1 volt as battery discharges its energy).

Best use: Clocks or similar low-drain, low-use devices.

Estimated shelf life (68°F/20°C): 3-5 years.

Pros:

Cheap.

Cons:

Shortest life of any battery.
Not recommended for extended use in outdoor electronic devices.
Not stocked at REI.

Rechargeable Batteries

Rechargeable Batteries Quick-reference Guide (PDF Download)

Nickel-Metal Hydride (NiMH)

As the name suggests, a NiMH battery consists of:

Nickel (typically nickel hydroxide; used for the cathode/positive electrode) an alloy (a mixture of metals or metal mixed with other elements; used for the anode/negative electrode) potassium hydroxide (an alkaline) as an electrolyte.

NiMH batteries have supplanted nickel cadmium (NiCd) batteries as the preferred cylindrical rechargeable battery. They offer higher energy capacity (up to 50% more) than NiCd batteries and avoid the high toxicity of cadmium.

Volts: 1.2 (steady voltage is generally sustained throughout a cycle, dropping to 1.1 before a charging cycle is complete).

Estimated number of recharging cycles: 150 to 500, maybe more, perhaps fewer.

Self-discharge rate: Loses 1% (or more) of stored power per day, roughly 40% per month.

Maintenance: Recharge whenever energy capacity drops 30% to 50% below its peak capacity. If left unused, it should be recharged every 1 to 2 months. Performs best over the long haul if used frequently. After many months or years of disuse, NiMHs may require a "conditioning" cycles (an option found on "smart" chargers) to revive its usefulness.

Storage: Store fully charged at 60°F/15.5°C.

Best use: High-drain devices (digital cameras, flash units) or devices that experience prolonged or continuous use (GPS receivers). Not recommended for items that are rarely used or infrequently inspected, such as smoke detectors or a flashlight in an emergency kit.

Pros:

Delivers energy capacity at a more constant rate (technically, a flatter discharge rate) than single-use batteries—for example, the light from a headlamp using alkaline batteries starts brightly and progressively grows dimmer. With NiMHs, the light level remains stable due to the steady voltage delivered by rechargeable batteries.
Delivers substantially more current (electron flow) than an alkaline battery, boosting its performance when servicing high-drain devices.
Energy capacity is up to 50% higher than NiCd batteries.
No measurable "memory effect" (explained later) that NiCd batteries exhibit.
Performs reasonably well in colder weather.
Better long-term value than single-use batteries.
Recyclable.

Cons:

Fairly fast rate of "self-discharge" (loss of power when not in use)—idle NiMH batteries may lose between 1% and 5% of their stored power in a day, between 30% and 40% in a month (and potentially more in warm conditions).

Should not be stored in very warm areas (affects longevity).
Moderately expensive initially.
Must be charged before first use.
Accommodates fewer recharging cycles than NiCd batteries.

Should be charged every 1 to 2 months. Energy capacity declines by 10% to 15% after 100-plus recharges.
Performance may diminish if dropped or handled roughly.

Notes: Best when charged in a "smart charger" designed for NiMH batteries. Some specialized chargers can restore NiMH batteries in 15 minutes. One innovative NiMH battery can be recharged by plugging it into a computer's USB slot.

Precharged NiMH

Also called "hybrid," "ready-to-use" or "low self-discharge" batteries, this NiMH battery comes precharged in its package so it's ready for action. It offers a very low self-discharge rate (power loss when not in use), which makes it best-of-breed in the rechargeable category for cylindrical batteries (AA, AAA, C and D cells).

Volts: 1.2 (steady voltage is generally sustained throughout a cycle).

Estimated number of recharging cycles: 150 to 500, maybe more.

Self-discharge rate: Much better than standard NiMH batteries, roughly 10% to 20% over 6 months.

Maintenance: If left unused, should be recharged every 6 to 9 months. Benefits by being used frequently.

Storage: Store fully charged at 60°F/15.5°C.

Best use: High-drain devices (digital cameras, flash units) or moderate-drain devices that experience prolonged or continuous use (GPS receivers). Its lower self-discharge rate also makes it suitable for smoke detectors, though the batteries much be recharged every 6 months to optimize power.

Pros: Same as standard NiMH, plus:

Can go straight from the package and into your device.
Much lower self-discharge rate than standard NiMH batteries (making this design an excellent choice for headlamps or any device that may be actively used for a week, then left untouched for months).

Cons:

Moderately expensive initially.
Accommodates fewer recharging cycles than NiCd batteries.
Energy capacity declines by 10% to 15% after a few hundred recharges.

Nickel Cadmium (NiCd)

This is the ancestor of NiMH batteries. Contains cadmium, a highly toxic component.

Volts: 1.2 (steady voltage is generally sustained throughout a cycle).

Best use: Power tools; two-way radios; high-temperature situations.

Estimated number of recharging cycles: Up to 1,500.

Self-discharge rate: Loses 1% of stored power (or more per day), roughly 40% per month.

Maintenance: If left unused, should be fully discharged and recharged every 2 to 3 months. Performs best over the long haul if used frequently.

Storage: Store fully discharged at 60°F/15.5°C. Recharge before next use.

Pros:

Less expensive than NiMH batteries.
Accepts more charging cycles.
Very rugged.
Moderate self-discharge rate (approximately 20% in a month).

Cons:

Contains a highly toxic component (cadmium).
Less energy capacity than NiMH batteries (typically 50% less).
 Often vulnerable to "memory effect," which causes a shortened run time (a flaw that sometimes can be corrected by 2, 3 or more repeated cycles of full discharging-full recharging).

Lithium-ion

They're not yet widely available in the cylindrical shape of AA, AAA, C or D batteries, but battery insiders say they are on the horizon. Lithium-ion batteries today are more commonly found in the form of a slab, block or battery-pack. They are used extensively in mobile phones, single-reflex digital cameras, computers, camcorders and other consumer electronics.

Volts: 3.6 (with some variations).

Estimated number of recharging cycles: 500 to 1,000+.

Self-discharge rate: Very low, but age is the enemy of Li-ion batteries. Even if unused, the simple passage of time robs them of some energy capacity. The quantity of the loss varies according to the size and configuration of the battery.

Maintenance: Should recharged frequently (even after shallow discharges of 10% and 20%). It is considered impossible to overcharge most Li-ion batteries, since they are designed to stop accepting energy when fully recharged. Recharge whenever it reaches 50% of its capacity. No damage will be done to the battery, however, if it is fully discharged.

Storage: Store at roughly 60°F/15.5°C, either fully charged or at 50% of capacity (opinions vary on this topic).

Best use: Notebook computers, camcorders (some camcorders use NiMH batteries), mobile phones, single-lens reflex cameras, some bike lights.

Pros:

Offers the lowest self-discharge rate (less than 10% in a month) of any rechargeable battery.

Cons:

More expensive.
Even if left unused, is negatively impacted by age.

Alkaline

Rechargeable alkaline batteries exist, but as their limitations became known, interest in them quickly flamed out. They can accommodate only a small number of recharging cycles (from 10 to perhaps a few dozen) before their usefulness is exhausted. They are also relatively expensive. REI regards them as a failed design and does not stock them.

N Cells

Created for use in extra-small devices. Available in both single-use and rechargeable models.

Volts: 1.2-1.5.

Pros: Small and light.

Cons: Limited energy capacity, requiring more frequent replacement.

Rechargeable Batteries: Q&A

Q: How often should batteries be recharged? What is the best way to store them?

A: Here's some pure-gold advice: Before using either a rechargeable battery or a charger, read and follow the manufacturer instructions. Still have questions? Contact the manufacturer.

Beyond that recommendation, here are the prevailing points of view (though opinions vary) on strategies for recharging and storing mainstream rechargeable batteries:

NiMH batteries (including precharged/hybrid varieties):

   Can be recharged at any time, no matter what level of energy capacity they retain.
   Periodically, it's OK to fully discharge and recharge batteries. This is known as "conditioning." See the next question for details.
   To begin a prolonged period of storage, all NiMH batteries first should be fully recharged.
   If left unused for long stretches, recharge accordingly:

Standard NiMH batteries: every 1 to 2 months

Precharged NiMHs batteries: every 6 to 9 months

NiCd batteries:

   Best maintained when completely drained before recharging is attempted.
   It is possible you to reduce the performance capabilities of NiCd batteries if they are recharged before being fully exhausted.
   Doing so could result in the dreaded "memory effect"—a loss of energy capacity after a NiCd receives a charge in a partially depleted state. A NiCd battery tends to "remember" to only store the amount of energy it delivered during its most recent discharge.
   NiMH batteries demonstrate no measurable evidence of a memory effect.

For prolonged periods of storage, NiCd batteries should first be fully drained.

Lithium-ion batteries: Available for outdoor microelectronic devices, but are commonly found in computers, single-reflex digital cameras, mobile phones.

Recharge often, even if only a modest amount of energy has been drained.

Li-ion batteries are not vulnerable to a memory effect.

Avoid fully exhausting a Li-ion before recharging. Doing so won't ruin a Li-ion, but it is not viewed as a recommended practice.

If a fully charged Li-ion battery is attached to device that also uses household electrical current (a notebook computer, for example), no recharging current is applied to the battery. A battery's voltage must drop below a certain level before it will accept a recharge. In general, a Li-ion battery thus cannot be overcharged even if the device is plugged in and operated for a prolonged period. (Check your device's manufacturer instructions for its battery instructions.)

More charging cycles can be achieved if a Li-ion battery is recharged after shallow discharges (roughly 30% of capacity, which can be determined on devices that offer an energy capacity indicator or battery "fuel gauge"). If possible, avoid scheduling recharges after medium (50%) or full (90%-100%) discharges.

For ideal long-term storage, opinions vary. All experts recommend choosing a cool location (roughly 60°F (15.5°C). Some people in the battery industry say it is acceptable to store a Li-ion battery fully charged; others advise draining it to approximately 40% to 50% of its peak capacity prior to storage. In many cases, it is hard for the average consumer to know precise capacity levels, even with devices that offer a "fuel gauge" display. The consumer should simply make his or her best estimate.

Q: Is "conditioning" needed for all rechargeable batteries?

A: Not necessarily, though opinions can vary widely on this topic when it comes to NiMH batteries. Your best bet is to consult and follow manufacturer instructions.

Conditioning is the process of "deep-cycle exercise" for rechargeable batteries, where most (but not quite all) of the capacity is drained from a battery, then it is fully recharged. Many newer chargers that offer sophisticated features include a conditioning cycle that can be accomplished with the touch of a button. Here's some basic guidance:

Standard NiMHs: Condition batteries after 10 normal recharging cycles. Some industry insiders say to condition NiMHs every 3 months, particularly if the batteries have been left unused or if battery performance seems sluggish compared to past performance. Conditioning prevents the formation of a crystal within the cell that can reduce its life.

Precharged NiMHs Same as standard NiMHs; every 10 cycles or every 3 months.

NiCds: Every recharging cycle should be a conditioning event.

Lithium-ion: Not necessary. However if you have a Li-ion battery pack with a fuel gauge or capacity indicator, fully discharging and recharging the battery occasionally is considered a good idea. This allows the fuel gauge electronics will relearn its full-capacity levels and keeps the fuel gauge as accurate as possible over the life of the battery pack. At some point in normal use, many people commonly drain their Li-ion batteries to a near-nothing level, so the next charge serves as a "conditioning" cycle for the fuel gauge.

Tip: Conditioning is beneficial if a battery is frequently recharged after it gets regular use but only for brief intervals. Example: a security guard using short flashlight bursts during a nightly walk.

Q: How many charges can a rechargeable battery accept?

A: Based on customer feedback and manufacturer claims, my best guess for NiMH batteries is between 150 and 500. Maybe more, perhaps up to 1,000, according to some manufacturer claims. But maybe just a little over 100 if the batteries are poorly maintained. After 500 charges, even the most optimistic estimate puts a NiMH at 80% of its original energy capacity. If used constantly, a rechargeable battery will not last forever. A battery will lose some of its capacity with every charge. Various additional factors will influence its longevity:

the severity of its power drain (the irregularity of a strobe-flashing camera vs. the steady, gentle pull of an energy-efficient headlamp)
the frequency of discharges the temperatures in which it operates (extreme cold or heat are no friends of batteries) the pattern of recharging it experiences.

Q: Are all chargers created equally?

A: Not quite. Some guidelines:

Do not attempt to recharge a NiMH battery in an older, timer-based NiCd charger, which could cause overcharging.
Likewise, do not attempt to recharge an older NiCd battery in a charger designed for NiMH batteries.
So-called "smart" chargers are preferred. Smart chargers are equipped with microprocessors that automatically shut off the flow of energy when batteries reach a full charge. Some can also supply a "trickle charge" to keep energy levels topped off until the batteries are needed for use. In some cases, chargers sold with rechargeable batteries are very basic, or "dumb" chargers that lack auto shutoff and other features. This requires the user to be a vigilant observer during a charging cycle to ensure batteries do not overheat.
For NiMH batteries, "quick" chargers are preferred over slow "overnight" chargers. Quick chargers often get the job done in less than 4 hours. (On average, 3 to 6 hours are needed.) It is generally believed rechargeable batteries last longer if charged with higher currents.
Older overnight chargers take as long as 12+ hours and may not automatically shut off the flow of energy when a battery's charge is fully restored. This puts batteries at risk of overcharging and damage. Signs of overcharging include excessive heat in the batteries and leakage.
Some newer "rapid" chargers (using technology called In-Cell Charge Control, or I-C3) refuel NiMH batteries in as little as 15 minutes.
If a set of rechargeable batteries has been idle only days or a few weeks, it is wise to top off its charge just before putting it into use.
One clever type of NiMH battery can be recharged using the USB slot of a computer.
Never attempt to recharge a single-use battery (alkaline, lithium, heavy duty). Note: Some specialized alkaline batteries have been designed to be

rechargeable, but they accept only a limited number of recharges and are not recommended.

If a NiMH has been stored unused for years, it may require more 2 or 3 recharge-discharge cycles (conditioning) to fully activate the electrolyte. If possible, use a *q*uick charger rather than a rapid charger in this situation. Most smart chargers offer a conditioning cycle.

Conditioning may also help revive a rechargeable battery that is exhibiting sluggish performance or abbreviated charges. If your charger lacks a conditioning feature, a local electronics shop may be able to assist you.

The terms used here to describe chargers—slow or overnight (12+ hours), quick (3 to 6 hours), rapid (15 minutes), smart (microprocessor-equipped)—are not universally found in manufacturer product descriptions. Look for time claims of charging cycles to determine a charger's capabilities.

Q: Can batteries be left in a charger for long stretches of time?

A: Refer to the instructions that accompany your specific charger. With newer chargers, particularly those with an automatic shutoff feature, the answer may be yes. Most battery experts, however, caution against leaving any battery in any charger for longer than a day.

Q: Should batteries feel warm during recharging?

A: All NiMH and NiCd batteries will grow warm during recharging. (Interestingly, lithium-ion batteries do not.) Note: Batteries may feel very warm in rapid (15-minute) chargers. In slower chargers, though, excessive heat Is a sign of potential trouble. If you notice leakage, terminate the charging process.

Q: What are ideal battery-charging conditions?

A: Room temperature; somewhere close to 68°F (20°C). Temperature extremes, particularly cold conditions, are tough on batteries. (It makes the electrolyte sludge-like.) And operating rechargeable batteries in very warm conditions will reduce the duration of their performance.

Battery Capacity Ratings

Brace yourself: This section will get a little technical

Capacity ratings (which, admittedly, are sometimes difficult to locate) are presented as milliamp hours (mAh). An ampere (amp) is the basic unit for measuring electrical current. A milliamp equals 1/1000th of an amp.

The mAh number indicates how many amps (how much current) a battery can supply over a given period of time. It's sort of the gas gauge of a battery's fuel tank. The higher the number, the more likely the battery will deliver prolonged performance.

Typical AA NiMH Ratings:

Standard NiMH: 2,500 mAh

Precharged NiMH: 2,100 mAh

This means the standard NiMH battery offers greater overall capacity than the precharged NiMH, and so it may be able to perform longer.

If both sets of batteries are charged at the identical time, the higher-rated standard NiMH will contain more energy than the precharged NiMH. So, for example, if you have hundreds of photos to shoot at a wedding and you want all the battery power you can get, the standard NiMH is probably your better choice. The precharged NiMH, meanwhile, will perform better when the period of use extends over weeks or months—say, for a backpacker on a hike lasting a week or longer.

Is a battery with a higher capacity always the better choice? Not necessarily, says Patricia Bennett, a Senior Engineer of Rechargeable Technologies at Rayovac. Since consumers typically equate higher numbers with higher performance expectations, battery-makers are eager to market batteries with ever-higher capacity ratings—up to 1,000 mAh for AAA batteries and 2,900 mAh for AAs. But as capacity increases, cycle life (the number of times you can recharge batteries) tends to decline.

"Depending on type of use, a 2,500 mAh cell without charge-retention technology [i.e., not a precharged battery] may only be good for 150 to 200 cycles," says Bennett. "To achieve capacity higher, changes have to be made that affect the cycle life. A 2,100 mAh battery used the same way may last for 500 or more cycles."

Note: Single-use batteries such as alkalines also are given mAh ratings, though manufacturers rarely include these ratings on product packaging. For a variety of technical factors, mAh ratings for single-use and rechargeable batteries are usually incompatible, sort of an apples-and-oranges thing. Thus comparing ratings of contrasting battery types is rarely helpful.

Example: An alkaline battery may be rated to 3,000 mAh. But if it is used to power a high-drain device such as a digital camera, its capacity is drained quickly. A NiMH battery rated 2,500 mAh, with its inherent ability to prolong the length of its discharge cycle, will outperform an alkaline in a camera. The exception: If the NiMH battery has not been properly maintained, needs conditioning or is very old.

(Technical note: Voltage pertains to the force that pushes electrons through a battery, not the battery's capacity.)
Battery Tips

Do not attempt to simultaneously recharge batteries of different capacities, different brands or different ages. Do not use batteries of different brands or different ages together.
Do not put single-use batteries in a refrigerator or freezer.
Some people in the battery industry assert that placing charged NiMH batteries in a freezer, if well-packaged to avoid collecting moisture, will enable them to retain a high percentage of stored energy. Frozen batteries should be restored to room temperature before usage. Other experts discourage the use of refrigeration or freezing for any batteries.
This tip was previously stated, but it's worth repeating: If left unused for long stretches of time, recharge standard NiMHs every 1 to 2 months, precharged NiMHs every 6 to 9 months.

Remove batteries from devices if they will be left unused for months at a time. This prevents a device from exerting a tiny drain on the batteries even though the device is inactive.

Remove single-use (non-rechargeable) batteries from a device when they are being powered by household AC current. Doing so spares the batteries from any tiny drain on their power reserves by the device.

Do not store batteries, particularly single-use batteries, in locations where heat can become intense, such as car trunks, attics or garages.

Avoid tossing batteries into a drawer, briefcase or bag where they may contact metal objects such as coins or paper clips. Doing so may cause a short or it could negatively affect a battery's polarity.

Never put batteries into a fire. Doing so could cause them to rupture and spill their contents. Also: Avoid tossing them into a metal container where heat could build up.

Solar Chargers (and Other Alternatives)

This fast-evolving product category offers the promise of portable power as long as you have a line of sight to the sun.

Typically, watch batteries are tiny, button-shaped lithium batteries that in most cases require a professional's touch for proper installation. Often they must be carefully placed into small spaces where misguided probing could damage a device's circuitry.

Many manufacturers of watches, altimeter and heart rate monitors will void the device's warranty if a consumer attempts to replace the batteries. Others tout "consumer-replaceable" batteries.

Usually no guesswork is involved in selecting a battery for these devices, since the devices can only accommodate batteries of a specific size.
Recycling/Disposal

Imagine this: The U.S. Environmental Protection Agency estimates that Americans purchase nearly 3 billion dry cell batteries each year. This means on average every American discards 8 batteries per year. Here's how to lessen your impact:
Rechargeable Batteries

Many communities allow single-use batteries, made without mercury since 1996, to be placed in household trash. One notable exception is California. The state still regards all batteries as hazardous waste and requires them to be either recycled locally or taken to:

A household hazardous waste disposal facility

A universal waste handler (e.g., storage facility or broker)

An authorized recycling facility.

Are batteries truly recycled—meaning that their materials are reclaimed for use in the manufacture of other products? Rechargeable batteries are definitely recycled. It's a different story for single-use batteries, though. While recycling technology is available, it is rarely used because little economic incentive exists to use it.

Your best move for depleted single-use batteries? Contact your community's waste-disposal company for guidance. Some electronics stores may collect batteries.

Well that is all for our discussion on batteries and I know it is a lot of information to digest and I don't expect you to remember it all. It is best to keep a copy of all of this valuable information at hand so you can refer to it as needed.

Let's move on now to protecting all of the items you'll be using batteries and power supplies in.

Electronics: Protection in the Outdoors

Phones, GPS, satellite messengers and radios serve as a lifeline for many outdoor enthusiasts.

To stay connected, how can you ensure your devices survive the hard knocks of human error and the whims of Mother Nature? Here are some tips that will help.

Protective accessories range from simple to deluxe:

Zip-seal food bags: For the cost of a few pennies, a sealable food bag creates an affordable, disposable layer of protection from light rain and splashes. You can usually use a touchscreen through the plastic. Since they're less-than-crystal-clear, though, they tend to blur photos and add glare.

Soft cases: Sized to fit many devices, these offer a more durable form of submergible protection. Clear panels allow reliable touchscreen and camera use. Some models feature waterproof headphone jacks, built-in flotation and tie-down points. Shop REI's selection of soft cases. (Note: Soft cases are categorized alongside hard-sided cases.)

Smartphone cases: These form fitting, device-specific cases deliver low-profile protection from drops, shock and scratches while preserving full access to touchscreens, buttons and ports. Some models add crush resistance and waterproof protection.

Hard-sided cases: The Fort Knox of protection options, these watertight containers can resist just about anything. Many come with customizable linings to cradle delicate items. They are ideal for storage and transport, but don't offer the quick access and functionality of other options.

Electronics damage is mostly caused by impact, water, and dust. "Your phone is probably the most critical device to protect," For protection against these hazards, I recommend using a device-specific case. It helps protect your phone from water, drops, grit and snow, all while preserving full access and functionality.

Tips From The Field

Even small amounts of moisture can wreak havoc. Make sure you thoroughly dry all your gear whenever you even suspect that it has come in contact with moisture. Avoid using devices during sudden temperature and humidity increases that create condensation and fogging, such as coming into a ski lodge from the slopes or going out into tropical heat from an air-conditioned room.

If there's even a chance of your phone getting wet, it goes into the case. This is nice because you can still use your phone and even make a phone call with the soft case on. However, taking photos may not work as well if the plastic isn't totally clear.

Consider weatherproof gear. Buy rugged, weatherized gadgets for most outdoor uses. I bought a waterproof POV like the GoPro camera action cam. Although it is a little extra money, it makes underwater shots pretty cool.

Keep your phone in a zippered pocket. take a no-nonsense approach to protecting your phone from going overboard or suffering saltwater damage. I highly recommend a zippered clothing pocket for phone storage around water. I've seen a couple phones take a dip by simply falling out of pockets. I use my headphones for most of my calls. That way the phone stays protected in my zippered pocket and I have my hands free to hook and net a fish!

Quick Tips

On hot, sunny days, keep your gadgets in the shade. Many electronic gadgets can be damaged by prolonged heat.

When in camp, keep all your portable electronics organized and secure in one protected place, such as a clean, dry cooler.

Drying a device in rice

If your device gets wet, don't try to turn it on until it's completely dry. Placing it in a container of dry rice or silica gel can help absorb lingering moisture. (If you do succeed in reviving your phone, be sure to back up your information right away. Corrosion may still develop later on.)

If it's been exposed to dry sand or dust, a few blasts from a can of compressed air can help clean it out.

You're going to need your phone in an emergent situation and that is why I have gone into depth as it relates to protecting it. There are of course other electronics such as your radios, hearing aids etc. that you must ensure remain high and dry in an emergency. Common sense should walk you through most any situations you might come upon so go slow, take your time to develop a useable plan and then exercise it each time you believe there might be (or actually is) a circumstance in which your valuable equipment could be damaged by the elements.

Lets talk about staying warm and dry.

Regardless of what circumstance has put you out into the cold cruel world you are going to need to be warm and dry. Along with that you'll need a way to cook the food you've managed to take with you when you left the place that suddenly, and perhaps without notice, has left you without a shelter in which you can comfortably stay. That being said we should now move on to exploring making a fire that could save your life and also the lives of those with you.

Most people believe that they'll be able to simply flick a lighter or strike a match and fire will be theirs for the asking. Unfortunately that isn't always the case and if you're not prepared to use some methods of making the fire you need it could be a very cold and uncomfortable time in the outdoors during a time of crisis. Let's explore FIRE.

How to Build a Campfire

For many, the campfire is a beloved and indispensable outdoor tradition—a kinetic, luminous, dreamlike force of nature that for generations has served as the centerpiece of backwoods gatherings.

Lets go through the key steps for building a successful campfire, as well as fire etiquette tips, whether you're car camping or backpacking or whatever the case might be.

Finding or Building a Fire Ring

Campgrounds: Build fires only in designated fire rings, grills or fireplaces. Most developed campgrounds have some version of these. Using a fire ring will lesson your impact and keep your fire contained.

Always check with the campground operator to make sure fires are permitted. In some areas, severe dry periods can cause campfires to be prohibited even in campgrounds.

If you're car camping in an undeveloped site, check in advance with the agency that administers the land (U.S. Forest Service, Bureau of Land Management, etc.). A campfire permit may be required. Of course in an emergency there might not be anyone to check with so use your best judgement as it relates to your survival.

Evaluate the site before starting a fire. If the site is brushy or has low-hanging branches, keep your fire small or skip it altogether. In dry conditions, fly-away embers could easily ignite a wildfire.

Backcountry: In backcountry areas where fires are permitted, use an existing fire ring if one has been left behind. Build a new one only in emergency situations and, if the situation permits, dismantle it when you are done. If one already exists, clean it out before you depart.

Clear away all flammable material from your fire pit. Ideally, the base of your fire should be sand or gravel or mineral soil (often found in streambeds or on gravel bars). Intense heat can sterlize healthy soil, so choose your site conscientiously.

An alternative to a fire ring is a mound fire. Using your sanitation trowel, build a circular, flat platform of mineral soil (sandy, light-colored, nonfertile dirt) about 6-8 inches high. Use this as the base for your fire. Ideally, build this platform on a flat rock. You can easily disperse the mound when you're finished.

Gathering Fire Wood

To burn a successful fire, you'll need three types fuel: tinder, kindling and firewood.

Tinder includes small twigs, dry leaves, needles or forest duff.
Kindling consists of small sticks, typically less than one inch around.
Firewood is any larger piece of wood and is what will keep your fire going long into the night.

Campgrounds: Use only local firewood. Nearby stores often carry firewood, and sometimes campground hosts offer bundles of firewood or kindling for sale.

Do not bring wood with you if you're traveling from more than 50 miles away. Campgrounds may even ban bring-your-own firewood regardless of the distance you travel. Why? To avoid introducing troublesome insects into a forest.

Call the campground or a local ranger office in advance for information and advice.

Backcountry: If you forage for firewood, gather only downed wood far from your site. Never cut live trees or break off branches from standing trees, even dead trees. Birds and wildlife make use of dead branches and snags.

Do not gather or burn pieces thicker than an adult's wrist. This is because thick chunks of wood are rarely allowed to burn completely and are typically left behind as blackened, unsightly scraps.

Remember to follow Leave No Trace principles when gathering wood.

Building a Campfire

Kindling and firewood can be assembled in a number of different ways. Popular styles include the teepee, log cabin and upside-down (or pyramid).

Teepee: Start with a small cone of kindling around a few handfuls of tinder that are loosely piled in the center of the fire ring. Once the fire is going strong and the temperature increases, you can add larger logs a few at a time as needed.

Log cabin: Place two larger pieces of firewood parallel to each other and with some room in between to form the base of your structure. Then, turn 90 degrees and place two slightly smaller pieces on top and perpendicular to form a square. Place plenty of tinder inside the square. Continue adding a few more layers of firewood around the perimeter, getting a little bit smaller with each layer. Finish with a layer of kindling and tinder across the top. Remember to leave space between logs so the fire can get plenty of oxygen.

Upside down (pyramid): Start with three or four of your largest logs side-by-side on the bottom layer. Turn 90 degrees and then add a second layer of slightly smaller logs on top. Continue alternating a few more layers in this manner, getting smaller as you go. Place your kindling and tinder on top.

Lighting a Campfire

Light the tinder with a match or lighter. Using fire starter that is designed to easily ignite can help the tinder catch the flame. (Be sure to carry waterproof matches and firestarter. Fire-making materials are considered one of the Ten Essentials.)

After lighting the tinder, blow lightly at the base of the fire to provide oxygen, which will help increase the intensity of the flame and further ignite the wood.

As the fire burns, move embers to the center to burn them completely. Ideally, you should reduce them to white ash.

Extinguishing Your Campfire

Extinguish all fires by pouring water on them, stirring the ashes, then applying more water. Repeat as often as needed. Ashes should be cool to the touch before you leave the site. Be utterly certain a fire and its embers are out and cold before you depart.

Never leave a campfire unattended!

Cleaning up Your Campfire

Burn trash items only if they can be fully consumed by fire and turned to ash. Do not attempt to burn plastic, cans or foil. If you do burn something that's not fully consumed, collect the remains when the fire is out and either pack it out or put it in a trash receptacle.

When you're in the backcountry, pack out any trash found in your pit. Extract any charcoal pieces left inside your ring, carry them away from your site, crush the chunks, then scatter the remnants and dust throughout a broad area. Dismantle any structure you might have built and ensure that the fire is completely out before you leave the area.

You Are Dry Thanks To Your Fire. But, Are You Really Warm?

Here's How To Dress For Survival.

Layering Basics

Layering your clothing is a tried-and-true way to maximize your comfort in the outdoors. The beauty of this simple concept is that it allows you to make quick adjustments based on your activity level and changes in the weather.

Each layer has a function. The base layer (against your skin) manages moisture; the insulating layer protects you from the cold; the shell layer (outer layer) shields you from wind and rain. You simply add or subtract layers as needed.

Your Base Layer: Moisture Management

Power Dry base layer

This is your next-to-skin layer. It helps regulate your body temperature by moving perspiration away from your skin.

Keeping dry helps you maintain a cool body temperature in the summer and avoid hypothermia in the winter. If you've ever worn a cotton T-shirt under your raincoat while you hiked, you probably remember feeling wet and clammy, even though you weren't getting wet from the rain itself. Cotton is a fabric that retains perspiration and can leave you chilled.

For outdoor comfort, your base layer should be made of merino wool (popularized by brands such as SmartWool, Ibex and Icebreaker), synthetic fabrics (polyesters such as Polartec Power Dry® or Patagonia Capilene®) or, for less-active uses, silk. Rather than absorbing moisture, these fabrics transport (or "wick") perspiration away from your skin, dispersing it on the outer surface where it can evaporate. The result: You stay drier even when you sweat, and your shirt dries faster afterwards.

Examples: A base layer can be anything from briefs and sports bras to long underwear sets (tops and bottoms) to tights and T-shirts. It can be designed to fit snugly or loosely. For cool conditions, thermal underwear is available in light-, mid- and expedition-weights. Choose the weight that best matches your activity and the temperature.

Your Middle Layer: Insulation

The insulating layer helps you retain heat by trapping air close to your body.

Natural fibers such as wool and goose down are excellent insulators. Merino wool sweaters and shirts offer soft, reliable warmth and keep on insulating even when wet. For very cold and dry conditions, goose down is best. It offers an unbeatable warmth-to-weight ratio and is highly compressible. Down's main drawback is that it must be kept dry to maintain its insulating ability. A new innovation—water-resistant down—promises to change this.

Classic fleece such as Polartec® 100, 200 or Thermal Pro polyester and other synthetics such as Thinsulate® provide warmth for a variety of conditions. They're lightweight, breathable and insulate even when wet. They also dry faster and have a higher warmth-to-weight ratio than even wool. Classic fleece's main drawbacks are wind permeability and bulk (it's less compressible than other fabrics).

Like thermal underwear, fleece tops are available in 3 weights:

Lightweight for aerobic activity or mild climates.
Midweight for moderate activity or climates.

Expedition-weight for low activity or cold climates.

Examples: For high-energy activities such as cross-country skiing, cycling or running, choose lightweight fleece (Polartec 100 or Power Dry) to avoid overheating. For cold conditions, try thicker fleece such as Polartec 200 or 300.

Wind fleece such as Polartec WindPro® polyester or Gore WindStopper® adds a high level of wind resistance to fleece. How? It uses a hidden membrane that does not affect breathability.

Your Shell Layer: Weather Protection

The shell or outer layer protects you from wind, rain or snow. Shells range from pricey mountaineering jackets to simple windproof jackets. Most allow at least some perspiration to escape; virtually all are treated with a durable water repellent (DWR) finish to make water bead up and roll off the fabric.

An outer shell is an important piece in bad weather, because if wind and water are allowed to penetrate to your inner layers, you begin to feel cold. Furthermore, without proper ventilation, perspiration can't evaporate but instead condenses on the inside of your shell.

Fit is another consideration. Your shell layer should be roomy enough to fit easily over other layers and not restrict your movement.

Shells can be lumped into the following categories:

Waterproof/breathable shells: The most functional (and expensive) choices, these are best for wet, cool conditions and alpine activities. Shells using laminated membranes such as Gore-Tex and eVent offer top performance; those using fabric coatings are a more economical alternative. Shells are categorized by REI as either rainwear, which emphasizes low weight and packability, or mountaineering wear, which is more abrasion-resistant and has additional features.

Water-resistant/breathable shells: These are best for light precipitation and high activity levels. Less expensive than waterproof/breathable shells, they're usually made of tightly woven fabrics (such as mini-ripstop nylon) to block wind and light rain.

Soft shells: These emphasize breathability. Most feature stretch fabric or fabric panels for added comfort during aerobic activities. Many offer both shell and insulative properties, so they in effect combine 2 layers into 1. Soft shells include cold- and mild-weather options.

Waterproof/non-breathable shells: These economical shells are ideal for rainy days with light activity (e.g., fishing, sports viewing). They are typically made of a sturdy, polyurethane-coated nylon which is water and windproof.

Insulated shells: Some outer shells have a layer of insulation built in—such as fleece—making them convenient for cold, wet conditions, but not as versatile for layering in fluctuating temperatures.

Layer correctly and you'll be far more comfortable while outside and sometimes even inside of a shelter that perhaps isn't quite as insulated or draft free as it should be or that you would prefer it being. Warm and dry is the goal during this trying time in your life. Do all you can to ensure that you and those around you remain warm and dry and life won't seem quite as bad as you might be led to believe by the circumstances surrounding you at the moment.

Health Concerns in the Outdoors

This list of common outdoor health problems includes preventative measures and remedies recommended by the NOLS Wilderness Medicine Institute. It will help you stay healthy when you're out doing your best to survive.

Sunburn Sunscreen

Sunburn, caused when your skin gets exposed to too much of the sun's ultraviolet light, is a common, but easily avoided, problem in the outdoors.

Prevention

All outdoor adventurers, but especially those who are fair-skinned, should wear sunscreen with an SPF (sun protection factor) of 30 or higher. The American Academy of Dermatology and the Skin Cancer Foundation recommend an application of sunscreen every 2 hours, even on cloudy days. They also offer these tips:

Minimize your exposure to the sun between 10am and 4pm. Potential for skin damage is greatest around noon (or 1pm during daylight saving time). At these peak-intensity hours, a fair-skinned person could suffer skin damage in less than 15 minutes.

Always shade your head, neck, ears and eyes, particularly at high elevations, where a thinner atmosphere allows more UV rays to reach your skin. Sand and snow can intensify the sun's impact. Some outdoor clothing comes with SPF ratings. Fabrics with tighter weaves help keep the sun off your skin.

Sunscreen should block both UVA and UVB rays (this is sometimes called "broad-spectrum sunscreen"). Examine product spec sheets or packaging to verify this level of protection.

Your sunglasses, too, should offer both UVA and UVB protection.

Check with your doctor to determine if any medications you are taking increase your susceptibility to sunburn.

Remedy: If you do get burned, soothe damaged areas with an aloe-based skin cream. Keep these areas covered for the remainder of your trip (either with clothing or a strong sunscreen) to avoid further damage. If the sunburn is serious and you experience persistent nausea, chills or fever, seek professional medical attention.

Sunscreen: How to Choose

Blisters

One blister, the product of friction that rubs skin back and forth in a concentrated area, can mar your outdoor experience and create problems that could eventually become serious.

Prevention:

Blisters are easier to avoid than they are to fix. Make sure you start every trip with footwear that is broken in and fits you well. Wear clean, properly sized socks. Also, consider wearing 2 pairs of socks—a lightweight wicking liner and a thicker cushioning sock—to lessen the chance of abrasion.

Tip:

On the trail, address foot discomfort as soon as it develops. A quick response can often stop a blister before it becomes serious. At the first sign of irritation, put a small patch of protective material—moleskin, 2nd Skin or even duct tape—over the affected area to minimize abrasion.

Remedy: If you know you are prone to blisters, consider applying moleskin to your typical "blister zone" before you hit the trail.

If a blister develops and walking becomes too painful, you could drain the blister by lancing it along its base with a clean razor blade or knife. Once this is done, soothe the area with some antibacterial ointment, then cover it with a patch of 2nd Skin (or similar product) plus a small adhesive bandage to keep the blistered area clean.

If the area is still sensitive, cut a doughnut-shaped cushioning patch out of Molefoam or duct tape and encircle the injured area. You may need to bulk up your circular pad with a number of layers to hold your sock and boot out away from the damaged area. This cushion will protect the area from further damage.

General Aches and Pains

Sore muscles, headaches and joint pain are a common occurrence on more strenuous outings.

Prevention:

The primary purpose of stretching before an aerobic activity is to increase body temperature. This increases blood flow so muscles can endure more force.

Dynamic stretching, such as a modest walk or jog, is generally preferred over static stretching for most people, though either can be useful if done carefully. For a hiker, the best warm-up is spending your first 10 or 15 minutes on the trail walking at a moderate pace.

If you feel the need to do some sort of pre-hike activity, you could try, for example, the straight-leg march. Begin by kicking one leg straight in front of you, with toes flexed skyward. Reach toward your airborne toes with your opposing arm. Drop that leg and perform the same motion with your opposite limbs. Aim for a half dozen or more repetitions.

Poison Ivy, Poison Oak and Sumac Plant

In most areas of the country, it is possible to run into one or more of these troublesome plants.

Prevention:

Learn how to recognize any dangerous plants that are common in the area you'll be exploring. Poison oak and ivy leaves grow in clusters of 3, so remember the old adage: If you see "leaves of 3, let it be." Be wary of touching anything foreign to you. Keep in mind that the oily, rash-causing resin found in poison oak and ivy—urushiol—remains present in the plants even during dormant winter months. Contact with a leafless stem in January can still spawn an itchy rash. Pre-exposure lotion can be helpful. If traveling in unfamiliar territory, consider carrying a lightweight, compact field guide to help you recognize plants.

Remedy:

Carry a small supply of hydrocortisone cream or another soothing, anti-inflammatory lotion to lessen the discomfort caused by skin irritations. Fluid from a rash-induced blister will not spread the rash. However, if the resin is not cleaned from clothing, boots, skin or tools, you can re-expose yourself or another person. It's the resin, not the rash, that spreads infection. A good first-aid manual will provide other useful tips on limiting the spread of rashes.

Biting Insects

Bug repellent

Mosquitoes, flies and other biting insects are an unavoidable part of nature. Fortunately, these bug bites are usually more of a nuisance than a health hazard.

Prevention:

Know your enemy and be prepared. This means identifying and avoiding the worst locations and times of year for bugs. It also means packing the right kinds of clothing (light-colored long-sleeve shirts, long pants, bug shirts, bug-net hats and so on) and using some form of topical repellent if necessary.

DEET-based insect repellents are the most effective against mosquitoes, though natural alternatives are available for those who prefer to avoid synthetic chemicals. DEET is not recommended for pregnant women or small children, especially those less than 1 year old. DEET will not hurt cotton, wool or nylon, but it can damage plastics and synthetic fabrics.

Clothing treated with permethrin, an EPA-registered chemical insecticide in use for decades, offers another effective line of defense. You can self-apply permethrin to your clothes or wear pre-infused garments.

Remedy:

First-aid products such as After Bite help relieve the swelling and itching caused by bug bites.

Tip:

Some people are allergic to certain insect stings. If you are, protect yourself by avoiding risky situations as much as possible and by carrying whatever medicines you need to counteract the reactions. Make sure everyone in your group knows about your allergy and what to do if you get stung or bit.

Stinging Insects

Bees, wasps, hornets and yellowjackets are additional winged threats you may encounter.

Prevention:

If you come upon a beehive or wasps' nest, leave the area quickly and quietly. In campgrounds, avoid brightly colored clothing, shiny jewelry or belt buckles, and scented cosmetics. If you or someone in your group is allergic to bee or wasp stings, make sure to visit a health care professional for preventative injections.

Remedy:

For a normal reaction to a sting (itching, redness and slight swelling) the following first-aid items may be useful: ice, baking soda, oral antihistamines (such as Benadryl, Chlortrimeton and Dimetane), epinephrine inhaler (such as Primatene), topical steroids (such as Cortaid or Lanacort) and local anesthetics (such as Benzocaine, Lanacane or Solarcaine).

Ticks

Ticks are nasty little arachnid bugs that can make you sick. While not all tick bites transmit Lyme disease or tick fever, it pays to be aware of these threats.

Prevention:

Avoid areas where ticks are prevalent such as vegetated areas (woods and grasslands) where small mammals live. Tuck in your clothing—shirts into pants, pants into socks. Do twice-daily checks of your skin and hair for ticks. DEET-based insect repellents on your skin and permethrin-based insect repellents applied to clothing can repel or kill some ticks.

Remedy:

If a tick is discovered, try to remove it as soon as possible. Using tweezers, gently grasp the tick by the head and lift it straight up and out. Wash the bite site thoroughly with soap and water, rubbing alcohol or iodine. Avoid Vaseline smothering, gasoline dousing, matchhead burning and other discredited folk remedies.

Note:

Ticks can only pass on their diseases if they are burrowed in your skin. Touching a tick or having one merely crawl on your skin is not dangerous.

Snakebites

Partially Hidden Snake:

While many snakes are harmless, a few (rattlesnake, coral snake, water moccasin and copperhead) have potentially lethal bites. Per the University of Maryland Medical Center, up to 8,000 people receive venomous snake bites each year in the U.S. (about a dozen or less typically prove fatal).

Prevention:

Avoid areas prone to snakes by checking your guidebook or asking a local ranger or guide for advice. Stay on trails or in well-groomed, open areas. Watch where you're going and listen. Be cautious and alert when climbing rocks. If you see a snake, don't antagonize it.

Remedy:

Never attempt to identify, capture or kill a snake, as this can easily result in a second bite victim. Follow these steps:

Calm yourself and the victim. Envenomation is not a given in a snakebite.

Immobilize the limb. Avoid compression or constriction of the extremity.

Transport victim to a physician or hospital for antivenom and supportive care.

Document the site and size of the envenomation to describe its progression to the physician.

Avoid unproven or discredited treatments that may harm the patient, such as tourniquets, ice, electricity, meat tenderizer, incision and suction.

Hantavirus:

Hantavirus is spread by the droppings, urine and saliva of contaminated rodents, particularly the deer mouse, cotton rat, rice rat and white-footed mouse.

Inhaling fumes or dust that carries traces of rodent excreta is the most likely way humans are exposed to the virus. This usually happens during activities such as cleaning a barn or cabin, but campers are potentially at some risk, too.

As pointed out by Dr. Paul Auerbach, author of the respected book Medicine for the Outdoors, a person infected by the virus has an incubation period of 1 to 5 weeks following exposure. Symptoms include fever, muscle aches, headache, cough, dizziness, abdominal pain, nausea and vomiting, and diarrhea for a few days. This is followed by difficulty breathing, mottled skin on the limbs, shock and, sometimes, bleeding. Up to 75% of victims may die.

Prevention:

Avoid any areas with excessive rodent activity: barns, old cabins or dusty, enclosed trail shelters. Take the following precautions:

Keep food and water covered and stored in rodent-proof containers.

Dispose of food clutter; spray any dead rodents, nests and droppings with disinfectant prior to handling (and wear gloves when you do).

Clean and disinfect cabins and other shelters thoroughly before using.

Don't make camp near rodent sites.

Don't sleep directly on bare ground.

Dispose, burn or bury garbage promptly.

Use only bottled or disinfected water for campsite purposes.

Remedy:

If you suspect that you or someone in your party has been infected with hantavirus, seek professional health care immediately. There is not yet any specific therapy beyond supportive care, although the antiviral agent ribavirin may prove useful.

Two is One. One is None: The Importance of Redundancy.

Having a plan for outdoor survival is important. But it's also important to have more than one tool available in the event that your equipment fails or is lost.

How many times have you had an excursion into the field where you have had a critical piece of equipment fail? Or maybe you lost or misplaced a tool? In a best case scenario, you might have been able to improvise. In the worst case, you had to head home early. But what would happen if you were actually in a survival situation? Having a back up for common items could enable you to continue your excursion and possibly even save your life.

I prefer to have a backup plan for four key areas: Shelter, Water, Fire, and Cutting

1. **Shelter** - Obviously, if you are actually camping, you are going to probably have a tent or tarp that you are using for your primary shelter. But if you are only on a day hike, fishing trip, or short term excursion, you probably will not have a formal piece of shelter equipment. I like to keep things simple and light. A poncho is great for this role. Nylon ponchos are my preference due to their strength and durability, but a PVC poncho will do in a pinch.

For a backup, you could consider a heavy duty trash can liner, preferably a 55 gallon one. The poncho or trash can liner can be quickly deployed to protect you from a sudden shower, or rigged as a shelter to protect from sun or wind. If you have the available resources, a shelter can be created from local material, but by having your own material, this will free you up for other tasks.

2. **Water** - We all know that you can't go around drinking untreated water in the backcountry. We have more options now than ever before for water

treatment. I prefer to carry a water purifier as my primary option, but it's important to have a backup.

A great lightweight option is a personal water purifier straw. This can be carried on any excursion and will not take up too much room. An additional option would be water purification tablets. If you have a container that is fire resistant, you can also boil the water, preferably for at least 15 minutes.

3. **Fire** - There are tons of options for fire sources. Waterproof matches are preferred if you are using matches as your primary source. You can buy them or make your own with paraffin, but be sure to use strike anywhere matches if you do. Torch lighters are also a great primary fire source, although disposable and zippo style lighters also work.

For a backup, you should consider items that won't be affected by water. Magnesium fire starters will not be harmed by water. Shave a small pile of magnesium shavings off the block and then use the striker to cast sparks onto the shavings. This is enough to light your tinder. Some people prefer to carry their own tinder, but be prepared to store it in a waterproof case. There are other options such as BlastMatch, Spark-Light, and the Swedish Fire Steel. I highly recommend practicing your fire building skills with both your primary and backup method before you ever head out. It can be difficult enough to build a fire with a new method under ideal conditions. The learning curve for a new method could be overwhelming if you wait until you are in a stressful situation.

4. **Cutting** - I hope you always carry some type of bladed tool when you venture out. My personal preference is a quality multi-tool, preferably lightweight, but functional. Having one with a pliers function has been extremely helpful at times in my experience.

Some people prefer a fixed blade knife. This is a personal preference. I have carried both folding lock back knives and fixed blades. A strong fixed blade knife can be used for chopping as well, but that can add weight and bulk.

For my back up, I prefer a simple light weight single blade folding knife. If I break or lose my primary blade, I've still got a way to cut. A small folding knife won't take up much room in your kit or pocket and will keep you going.

This is by no way a comprehensive list. I created this list as a simple reminder of the basic items that anyone can carry with minimal bulk. These items can all fit in a small pouch in your backpack or on your belt.

If you and/or your family finds themselves in an emergent situation then I believe it is important for each member to have their own emergency pack. If only one person has what could be needed and they are somehow separated from the others then the situation becomes even more severe than when it first started. Ensure that everyone has what he or she needs to survive and that, most importantly, they know how to use all of what is in the pack they are carrying.

The Rule of 3's:

In emergency situations, one of the biggest problems is to focus on what matters most. That's why in the field of emergency medicine, staff uses acronyms and steps like the "ABC's" to help them control panic and remember what they should do first, then second, etc...

It is always interesting to see how people react in emergency situations. And over the years, I grew to really love acronyms such as the Rule of 3's because of how they help people focus when the chips are down.

Survival is no different, we still need to control panic and prioritize our efforts. This is where the "Rule of 3's" comes in.

The Rule of 3's simply stated is you have:

3 minutes without AIR

3 hours without SHELTER

3 days without WATER

3 weeks without FOOD

So what does all this mean? It tells us where our priorities should be in a survival situation.

First, we should focus on all life threatening conditions making sure we'll still be breathing in the near future. Next, we should worry about shelter because more people die of exposure than any other incident in the outdoors. Next is water. And then finally food, which is last, not first. You would be surprised at how long a human can go without food (we're a little spoiled in modern society in the area of food).

Search and rescue statistics show most people are rescued within 72 hours, so if you handle the first 2 priorities, you're most likely going to make it.

If things do go longer, you know what's next -- water. And finally, last but not least, food. The "Rule of 3's" (just like the "ABC's") is a tool to help you control panic and remember in any survival situation what your steps are and what matters most.

Using What You Have: RV and Travel Trailers as Emergency Shelters.

I've made it pretty clear that if you expect to survive in an emergency situation regardless of whether it is man-made or nature related you have to be as fully prepared as possible at all times.

In today's mobile society many people have purchased and use regularly RV's and Travel Trailers. They are in fact as close to the best shelter solution you can have in an emergent situation. Of course there are some things to consider such as the availability of fuel etc. that you must be aware of but in general if you can park your vehicle somewhere and live in it for a period of time your chances of survival increase greatly.

Rv's offer shelter, a certain degree of warmth, security from others around you that might want to cause you harm and also, generally, have storage areas in which you can pre-prepare for an emergency or bug-out situation. When used wisely, packed correctly and made ready for travel at any given time RV's offer one of the best ways to survive.

Of course no one looks forward to dealing with disaster, but when it strikes unexpectedly, you can proceed with confidence if you are ready for the unpredictable. Everyone should be organized for the hurricanes, wildfire, or any calamity that requires you to leave your home and seek shelter. Hotels, and motels fill up quickly in emergencies, and most public shelters will not allow you to bring your pets. If you are fortunate enough to have a travel trailer, you can use it as an emergency shelter.

Get ready in advance

If you have ever lived where a hurricane, blizzard, or other severe weather is predicted, you know that the grocery store supplies deplete quickly. Even if you shop as soon as you hear the news, chances are all of the bottled water will be gone when you get there. Realistically, you need food and water for a week - and don't forget your pets. Plan simple meals, and purchase what is necessary. Use freeze-dried foods as much as possible.

Ensure that you have propane for cooking. Include cleaning supplies as you pack.

Remember to plan for where you are going. Even if your trip involves only a short drive to a friend or neighbor's house you must still prepare as though your trip will be hundreds of miles long. You never know, it just might be longer than you would ever expect.   Situations change, circumstances sneak up on you without warning and if you're not prepared it could spell disaster for you and those around you.

Pack clothing suitable for your climate, and the season. Store copies of all of your important papers in the RV in case you lose your home. Have a list of possible safe parking areas in the travel trailer

Keep your vehicle's gas tank filled up, and store extra gasoline to take with you. Maintain your RV in good mechanical condition, and check the fluids regularly. Remember to take a battery operated radio, and replacement batteries. You might put some games and books on board as well. If you have everything ready to go, you will save precious minutes when they count.

Everyone should have a job

Each person who will be evacuating in case of an emergency should have a job to do. Someone may be responsible for getting the pets into the RV. Another may be in charge of any medications. Assign a person to do a head count. You can probably think of other things that need to be on the list. Once a month schedule a rehearsal emergency where everyone is responsible for his evacuation chores.

Disasters can happen without warning. With some forethought, and preparation, you and your family will be ready for almost immediate evacuation. Plan, and keep your head.

Hunting to Survive: The First Time Out Is Never Good:

There are things that require a certain skill level to perform competently and hunting is no exception. Hunting game for food can keep you and your family alive for extended periods if you have the right skills. Learning how to hunt is critical for survival when you are lost in the woods or even when your city's infrastructure has been destroyed because of a disaster. You can find game in many urban areas or only a few miles outside of any city. You can expect to find geese, ducks, squirrels and pigeons in an urban environment.

Just because you have a hunting weapon does not mean you will be able to feed yourself. You must know how to use that weapon, in other words you must learn how to hunt. You will need to learn how to handle your weapon, and learn about the game you are hunting, where to find them, identify their tracks and then learn how to process the game once killed. There are several different types of weapons you can use but a firearm is probably the most versatile and accurate weapon for anyone just starting out.

To be successful and to prevent starvation you must develop your hunting skills before you are called upon to provide for yourself and family in an emergency. Stress and lack of skill is a recipe for failure in a survival situation. There are things you never attempt without the needed skills and hunting is one of those things.

Before you can have a successful hunt, it is crucial that you must practice with a weapon and strengthen your hunting skills. If you chose to use a bow and arrow, you should spend many hours practicing shooting targets so you are comfortable and proficient at shooting. Extra precaution must be taken with firearms and safety courses should be attended in preparation of hunting.

There are likely groups in your area that you can join to get training on archery, firearms, and setting traps. Seek out others with hunting skills through internet meetup groups, outdoor supply stores, and local clubs.

Once you are familiar with your weapon or method of hunting, you must get into the woods and hunt but in a controlled situation. You want to learn your skills before a disaster strikes so your failures while training will not have an impact on lives. It will take patience and trial and error to learn the game you are hunting. The investment you put into your hunting skills today will save lives in the future when you are called upon to provide food by hunting.

The Bow and Arrow as a Survival Instrument:

Archery is an ancient sport that is centuries old and uses arrows and an archery bow has quite an interesting history. In generations past, archery was critical for survival, yet almost died out in the modern world. How could this sport, which is really quite popular, go from one extreme to the other?

Long before man had gunpowder to power bullets and other weapons, a simple bow and arrow was all that separated early man from other beasts of the times. Since man was slow and defenseless as compared to other animals, he developed weapons. First came the spear, but he soon figured out how to make arrows that were propelled by a simple stick with a string tied to both ends - a bow.

This simple weapon helped ensure man's survival, as even the fastest animal was no match for the speed of an arrow - propelled by an archery bow. As the centuries passed, archery equipment was needed less and less, mainly due to the proliferation of modern inventions such as the gun. When the last of the American Indians were placed on reservations in the early 1900's, archery almost died in the U.S. as there was no real practical use for this ancient technology.

Technological developments such as the compound bow, which multiplied the force of a bow by using pulleys and a much stiffer bow material and arrows made of metals vs. stone propelled archery to a much higher plane of importance. While these improvements to the basics of archery occurred hundreds of years ago, their basic designs have carried over largely intact over the centuries.

New man-made materials such as fiberglass, plastics and graphite construction have contributed to huge improvements in performance as compared to archery bows of years ago. And, the resurgence of bow hunting as a serious sport, rather than using a gun, has given new meaning to the "art" of hunting, as bow hunters can't rely on the awesome power of a gun to bring down their prey.

Using a bow and arrow in an emergency situation is not only practical it is vital. Because the bow and arrow is silent you're much more likely to go unnoticed as you provide for your family. Drawing attention to yourself is never a good idea while trying to survive unless it is for the intent of being rescued. Stealth and silence could be the difference in whether you survive or starve in the wilderness waiting for things to settle down enough so you can return to your previous home location.

Learn how to use this valuable tool and survive. A gun is nice but the bow and arrow is proven, silent and deadly.

Sock It To Me!

I can pretty much guarantee that you have never considered socks to be a survival tool, right? Well, they are and we're going to discuss just how important they could be to your survival bag.

The nice thing about socks is that they are everywhere, and many people will overlook them in their rush to find items that were made explicitly for the needed function. Therefore, finding socks in a survival situation will not be that hard.

Socks go both ways when it comes to survival. On the good side, they are usually small and lightweight. This makes it possible to carry quite a few of them without weighing down a pack or tote. On the bad side, they are they are usually small and lightweight. Therefore, you need a lot of them if you have a bigger project planned. And you'll need to find heavy duty socks if you want extra thickness or bulk.

Besides just wearing them, I actually came up with some pretty creative uses for socks. But before we completely bypass just wearing them, let's do say something about just wearing them. If there's been a catastrophe of some kind, then taking care of your feet becomes very important. When all other modes of transportation are out, walking is the only remaining option. But it's pretty hard with sore or tired or infected feet. Because of this, it's important to keep your feet as clean and dry as possible. You should find all the socks you can and change them often. Wash them and hang them up to dry so that you always have a clean pair at hand. Feet sweat a lot, so try to have enough pairs to change at least once a day. More often is better, but if it's not possible, then be sure to remove your socks daily and check your feet. Wash the socks hang them to dry whenever you can.

First, if you don't have shoes, it's possible to put on several layers of socks in order to cushion your step. They will wear through rather quickly if you're walking on a rough surface such as cement. If this is the case, then hopefully you can have multiple pairs to use.

Second, while you're wearing your socks, it's possible to tuck small items into them for carrying. This frees up your hands or pockets for other things. I've seen people stuff money, tissues, nuts and screws, extra loose ammo, and even small food items into their socks to keep them safe. Unless the socks are really loose, these items won't fall out. However, they might slide down over time and slip under your heel. So a sock that fits snugly is best for this kind of use.

Third, clean socks are also great for straining liquids. Just pour the liquid in through the top and larger items will be filtered out while the liquid runs through. If smaller granules need to be filtered, like sand for instance, then you'd need a sock with a much smaller weave. The thicker the sock, the heavier the yarn will be, and hence the looser the weave. So, for straining smaller items, you should look for dress socks that have a smaller weave.

Fourth, socks with larger weaves work well for holding long items. For example, if a person has whittled some spears or arrows and wants to carry them, they can be slid inside a sock and poked through the bottom to hold them in place. We assume here that the person isn't actually wearing the sock, but just carrying it. In other words, if you're in a pinch, the sock can take the place of a quiver and the feet aren't the only place that can benefit from using socks.

Fifth, they make great hand warmers.

Sixth, use them as oven mitts when needing to move very hot or cold items.

Seventh, you can also fill socks with rice and heat them up to make a bed warmer. Or fill them with rice or sand and use them as a weapon.

Eighth, you can cut the top portion off of a sweat-type sock and stretch it out to use as a headband or wristbands.

Ninth, you can use it in place of a large rubber band. Socks actually make great holders for a lot of different types of items.

Ten is one that many people don't consider, and that's the actual thread or yarn used in the sock. If necessary, a sock can be pulled apart and the thread or yarn taken to be used for other things. If needing something pretty heavy-duty, a lot of socks would have to be undone and the various threads would have to be combined to add strength. But in a survival situation, we don't want to overlook any options.

Weapons Of Opportunity:

In your attempt to survive there could come a time when you have no "acknowledged" weapon available. Things like guns, knives etc. simply aren't around you for you to be able to use. In those cases you might have to revert to weapons of opportunity and that's what we'll discuss next.

A person who has the right motivation, talent and will to survive can employ almost any object as a weapon.

Anything can become a weapon when your mind is the real weapon. Governments can't ban it, customs can't confiscate it and the only time you don't have it is when you are asleep. This is the KEY lesson you should take away from this article.

In today's anti-weapons climate many times and in many locations it's impossible to carry a gun or knife (Courts, airports, etc). Even in your home at the time of a violent invasion you might not be close to your gun, or even knife.

Sometimes all you have left is your tactical creativity and your motivation and ability for thinking outside the box.

Your mind will always be your greatest weapon, not least of all because with your intelligence and ingenuity you can locate the most effective duel use objects to use as weapons during an assault. Your mind is a weapon, and with it you are never unarmed. Wherever you are I guarantee you you are surrounded by a multitude of potential weapons. Learn to spot them effectively.

While the will to use improvised weapons is often instinctive for the experienced fighter, the effectiveness of such improvised weapons can depend on how good an eye you have in not only quickly locating and choosing your improvised "weapon" but also on your ability to use that object in a way that will disable your attacker effectively (or allow you to escape the threat). And it is this ability that will increase only with proper training.

First a few thoughts on Natural Reactions:

Think of fights you might have seen yourself. What are the first natural reactions a person has when being attacked? First the person will put up his arms to block any attack, then they will instinctively grab for any object that can multiply the expediency of their own "god" given weapons (their body and limbs). Often one of the first such objects grabbed is a chair and it is used as a shield. If not a chair it will be another object that can be used as either a weapon or shield. It's an instinctive and natural reaction displayed by seasoned fighters and people with no experience in self defense alike.

Often the manner in which the attacked will use the object depends on their mindset and/or level of aggression and the situation itself. For example some people when attacked will grab a chair and only use it as a shield. Other more aggressive fighters will instinctively begin hitting their attacker with the same chair and thus using it more as a striking weapon than merely a shield. Using the chair or other object as a striking weapon will disrupt your attacker's ability from gaining direction, lead and control of the attack. While using the chair or other object as a shield can often be useful initially (especially in a surprise attack) you need to gain dominance and control rapidly through overwhelming force and aggression.

Often not much thought goes into such a split second decision in terms of exactly which object to grab for. There simply isn't enough time for someone who is being attacked to weigh up the potential effectiveness of one object over another. This will come with experience.
At the end of the day though, almost any object can be used as either a weapon or atleast a shield, some objects that I'm sure you would never have thought of as weapons or even shields. Obviously though, some objects are more effective than others.

The following is a list of a few possible objects you very well might have in your environment that could be employed as improvised weapons or shields:

The flashlight:

A favourite among many a self defense practitioner for years now. Wrap some 550 paracord around it and make a Koppo type weapon or use by itself. Either way it's a popular alternative weapon (and flashlight!). Can be used to momentarily blind an attacker or as an impact weapon. See specialist knowledge on how to use it most effectively.

Car antenna:

Listen up, in particular women who walk alone in car parks! You can quite quickly break off a metal car antenna and use it to fend off one or more attackers in a whipping action. The strikes can be very painful and effective and will likely at the very least stun and discourage an attacker from continuing. Remember, often these predators are looking for an easy victim. If you prove to the attacker that you'll be more trouble than your worth, he's quite likely to discontinue the attack and seek out someone who will give him less trouble.

Keys:

Not the easiest or most effective option in reality despite often being recommended by defensive instructors. Shouldn't be your first choice, however if you have nothing else at hand it's better than nothing. Hold key between middle fingers and use to punch with greater effect. Or can be used to scrape across attacker's face.

Steel Steel-toed Boots:

Often overlooked but very legal everywhere and a very painful alternative weapon. Kick attacker in the shins or groin. A real fight stopper with proper alm.

Pens:

As the saying goes, "The pen is mightier than the sword". Well, surely that was meant figuratively. In any case, when carrying a sword during your daily business is not a reasonable option (and I can't imagine it is for most people) a pen makes *q*uite a mighty alternative weapon. Another favorite among seasoned Martialists. Can be used as a stabbing implement or as a makeshift Kubaton. Hold in a pikal grip with your thumb on the clicker or blunt end and stab down or sideways repeatedly with the pointy end outwards. Hit to the liver, other soft appendages and neck for greatest effect. If you know how to use a Kubaton you know how to use a pen as a weapon. Choose a hefty strong metal pen like the now discontinued Rotring 600, a beefy hexagonal pen made of chrome-plated brass. Always legal, always useful for the intelligent and literate person for more than just self-defense, and a good alternative weapon for the concerned self defense practitioner.

The beer bottle, or other glass bottle:

Be careful with this one. Unlike in the movies DO NOT ever first break the bottle on the table thinking you'll be left with a sharp knife like weapon. You won't. In reality what you will be left with is a small piece of the bottle's neck. That's it. Nothing sharp protruding at any length and nothing you can use effectively as a weapon. In fact, for that matter, most of what you see on TV does not work, was never meant to work, and if you try it you'll probably be in big trouble.

You can still use a glass bottle as a weapon though, just don't break it on the table first, smash it directly in your attacker's face! Preferably use a glass bottle full of liquids, as an empty one will be far less effective.

Coffee mug or glass or ceramic cup:

Smash it across your attacker's face much like the glass bottle.

If you have hot coffee inside at the time, obviously splash it on his face. All the sudden you won't complain that McDonalds makes their coffee too hot. The hotter the better as an alternative weapon.

If there is alcohol inside your glass, throw it in your attacker's face. Aim for the eyes for stinging effect.

Carabiner:

An old army trick. Use a large one as a makeshift "knuckleduster". Works well. Punch and hammer fist your attacker's head and face. Preferably you would have a steel one, but an aluminum type will work well enough if need be.

A chair:

A chair, not only to keep lions at bay they can also keep your attacker at bay or shield you from a knife attack. They also make good larger improvised impact devices, although they are mainly best used as a shield.

Trash can lid:

Another great improvised shield. The trash can itself can be thrown at the BG and might at least give you time to escape or to employ a better weapon.

Dresser drawer:

That's right, if you're attacked in your bedroom immediately grab and pull out a drawer from the dresser. Can be used as a shield or even as an impact weapon, much like the laptop or book. Check out your drawers right now and see if they come out completely and easily. If they don't, try modifying them.

Walking cane/stick:

One of the best alternative weapons. Huge striking power. Easy to use and especially effective with modern Arnis Filipino stick fighting techniques. Always legal, always with you, always right in your hand ready to be used to strike, to disarm or to block an attack. It can however make you seem weaker or partially disabled, and thus can make you a more desirable victim or target to an attacker. Remember, predators target the weakest people, or in other words the people who they think will put up the least amount of fight. Keep this in mind and decide for yourself whether a walking stick is a good option. Certainly, in any case, if you carry a walking stick then do seek out combat stick training.

A padlock:

Devastating weapon, you can only hope to be lucky enough to have one handy. Slip your middle finger inside the steel loop with the rest of the padlock in your fist. Use as makeshift knuckleduster or fist-load. Or swing padlock at your attacker while holding it with one finger and the rest of padlock outwards. Aim for head, as the padlock would be too small to do damage to body.

Ashtray:

Usually a hefty solid weapon. Grab it like a frisbee and slam it into your assailant's head, face, or jam it in his neck or throat. Throw the cigarette butts and ashes in his face as a distraction.

Magazine:

Rolled up it can make an excellent impact weapon. Most effective using quick, strong, short strikes repeatedly to attacker's face and to other more sensitive areas due to the inherent lack of mass of the magazine.

Tie:

If you're a business man in a suit you've got an excellent flexible weapon or a possible garrot as part of you wardrobe. If your attacker is in fact the one wearing a tie you can use it to control or disorient him. Grab his tie and pull downwards hard.

Please note: This is one reason I generally advise people not to wear anything that doesn't break easily around the neck. It is too easy for someone to use it to control you during an attack, just as you can use the same tactic on someone else.

Laptop:

As was recently reported a celebrity used one as a weapon against a pushy paparazzi with great effect. Hold with both hands and slam into your attacker's face full force or push out and jab it into his face, neck or midsection with the sides/edges of the closed laptop. Can also be used to shield against an attacker's weapon or strike.

Clipboard:

Used much the same way as the laptop. Has thinner and so sharper edges, however on the other hand it also has less mass and might be less painful because of that.

A book:

Not only good for reading and learning. Used much the same way as the laptop and clipboard, although the book would have more heft than a clipboard.

Briefcase:

You're already holding it, and it has a secure handle. Swing it into your attacker's face/head or use as a shield. Push him away with the briefcase and escape. Open briefcase and take out other alternative weapons that have been mentioned here such as magazine, pen, etc.

Lamp:

You'll usually have a lamp nearby in your home. Grab it, and smash it across your attacker's face. Use the cord as a flexible weapon.

Fire Extinguisher:

Has been used before with great effect. Devastating power. Aim for head/ face. Makes an excellent shield too. Also spray contents directly onto attacker. It will at the least disorient him, it will often even hide your exit due to the cloud of white dust.

Put one in you car. You should have one in your car anyway for fire safety, but it might even save your life if you need to use it as a weapon.

Duct tape:

Not a weapon as such but makes good handcuffs to hold your attacker until the police arrive. Large zip ties are a good alternative to duct tape.

Light switch:

Darkness is a brilliant weapon under the right circumstances. If you are attacked by night, the light switch can be the best "weapon" for defense, without really being a weapon as such. Simply turn the lights off. Darkness is a tactical advantage for you, after all you know the layout of your own house while your attacker does not. You also know where you have other weapons and escape routes. Darkness could also simply give you the time needed to escape. Also, darkness will increase the blinding effectiveness of your flashlight if you are carrying one.

Clothing:

Are you wearing a coat or scarf? A coat or jacket can be used to shield yourself against an attacker's knife or other weapon. Wrap it around your weak arm, and hit and defend yourself with your strong arm and legs.

The long sleeves can also be used as a flexible weapon for choking or entangling limbs.

If on your bicycle:

Your helmet, tire pump, and flexible bike locks are potential impact devices.

Even the bike itself can act as an effective shield against an attacker. It will act as a good obstruction between you and him giving you time to escape. If need be it can even be thrown at the attacker.

Belt buckle:

A heavy brass or steel one. Can make a great impact weapon. Can even be swung at the attacker since it's attached to your belt.

Belt:

Even without a heavy buckle your belt can be one of the best flexible weapons available.

Sprays:

Any spray will do brilliantly. Think about it, what spray do you have around? Hair spray? Deodorant? Air freshener? Silicone spray? I personally have all and more of these sprays right here as I type this, aside from the hair spray. All these sprays will blind your attacker almost as well as pepper spray. If you're a smoker you probably have a lighter handy. Add a lighter in front of the spray and you've got an excellent flame thrower. I'm sure we all tried this when we were kids.

At the very least the spray can be used as an impact weapon if nothing else.

Comb:

Especially a metal comb.

Can be raked across an attacker's face repeatedly with good success.

Umbrella:

Always another favorite. The larger ones make a good impact weapon and improvised stick fighting weapon. Also a great shield a la Roman style when opened. Some of the full sized ones have a pointy bit protruding, perhaps 2 to 3 inches long, so while you shield yourself you can also push the opened umbrella forward into the attacker's face and body.

The smaller umbrellas are good too, however of course they are less durable and have less power due to lack of size.

Iron:

A great common household device. Can cause a lot of damage from use as a striking weapon, and again most irons have an electrical cord that makes a good flexible weapon as well.

A broom or mop:

Another long impact device. Can be used as a long staff for stick fighting techniques. Can also be used to hold the attacker at a distance.

Your car:

While it's not always justified to use deadly force in this way since it can be argued that if you're inside your car you are safe, if a gang of hoodlums or an angry middle eastern mob is surrounding your car, you've got 3000 pounds worth of effective weaponry on hand. At times deadly force can be justified depending on the situation including any disparity of force between you and the attacker(s) and the resulting danger you face at the time. Your main goal should be to escape in this case, but if necessary run a hoodlum over to affect your escape.

A phone:

Excellent impact device, very handy. A cord phone also makes a good flexible weapon if you're skilled in using one effectively.

Phones have been used many times as impact devices.

Coins:

Throw coins from your pocket into the face of your attacker. Another good diversionary tactic.

A packed roll of coins can also make a good fist-load and has been used many times as such.

Sports equipment:

Tennis racket, golf club, pool stick, the obvious and often used baseball bat, dumbbells, etc. All are excellent impact devices. Keep a few golf clubs and balls in your car even if you don't play. Or a baseball bat and glove and maybe some balls too in order to not raise the suspicion of LEO.

Watch:

Preferably a heavy steel dive watch. Take the watch off your wrist and wrap it around the fist you punch with (strong arm). The first punch should break the glass and subsequent punches could cut your attacker up. Even if the glass doesn't break and cut him it's still a good improvised impact device if need be.

Your voice:

Your voice can be a great improvised weapon wherever you are.

Verbally you can often stop, control or at very least influence the direction of an attack. Far too an extensive a subject to get into here. Learn about verbal commands and communication skills for defensive purposes/ redirection of attacker's violent behavior toward you. Sometimes known as verbal judo. Any good martial art or self defense system needs to address this subject.

---- One note on employing flexible weapons:

As you can see a number of the potential weapons I mentioned in this small list are flexible, for example the electrical cord and clothing. Please keep in mind that as with most flexible weapons, specialist knowledge in hand to hand combat is needed for most effective use. Flexible weapons simply aren't as straight forward as let's say a chair or even a book which will instinctively be used as a shield often even by people with little or no experience in self defense.

This is merely a small sampling of possibilities. It would be impossible to list for you all the possible alternative use "weapons"/objects you might come across that might be of great defensive use during an attack. The list would be too large, and no one can know what will be available to you in your specific environment at that time. Obviously some environments are richer in potential alternative weaponry than others. It's you're job to train yourself to identify these potential weapons out of any objects around you.

From now on look at the objects around you with a different eye. Look at objects in your surroundings through sort of a "weapons" filter. Specifically ask yourself, which ones can make an effective weapon? How would you use it? Will that object really cause hurt to your attacker and disable him, or is it really just a waste of time? Sometimes an object would make such a poor weapon that it's better to fight unarmed. Learn to accurately evaluate potential weapons in your environment.

No one can really instruct you or show you every object that has the potential to be used as a weapon. Above all it is a mindset that you will have to develop. Preparation and training is the best way to help guarantee a better chance for success in a self defense incident. But once you develop this situational awareness and survival mentality you'll be much better prepared to defend yourself in any situation than ever before, for you will have an instinctive understanding and application of self defense as a way of life.

Think outside the box, think like a fighter, like someone committed to self preservation and the defense of loved ones from societal predators.

Potential weapons are all around you.

It is now simply a matter of identifying them.

The 4 Pillars of Handgun Self-Defense

One of the most frequently asked questions in the realm of self-defense training involves the use of weapons, like guns and knives, for protection.

Here we are going to outline the four areas that make up a complete defensive handgun training program.

While most people, and subsequently most programs, focus on the shooting facet of gun training, there is actually much more to the subject. Just as any solid, well-structured, and complete self-defense program should include lessons on the care, selection, and safe-use of firearms if it is really to be of service to students in today's often violent world.

As I said, unfortunately, most so-called defensive handgun training courses only focus on shooting skills. I say "unfortunately," because shooting skills make up only one-quarter of the overall training that you should be learning if you're really going to be able to defend yourself in a dangerous self-defense situation involving firearms.

Before we look at what I call, the 4 Pillars of Defensive Handgun Mastery, you need to understand that, to truly be prepared - to truly be effective - when it comes to self-defense situations involving guns, there are three possible scenarios.

You could find yourself in a situation where:

You are armed but your assailant is not

Your assailant is armed and you are not, and...

Both you and your assailant are armed

And, of course, each of these situations includes variables such as when the weapon comes into play, distance between attacker and defender, and many more. All of these elements should be included in your training if you're serious about self-protection.

Keeping these three scenario-types in-mind, we can see that shooting skills, while vitally important, are not the only skills we will need if we want to survive a hostile attack. In fact, in 2-out-of-3 of the scenarios, shooting is either not an option or may not be a legally viable option.

So, what are the 4 pillars of defensive handgun training mastery that you should be focused on?

Here they are:

1. Basic skills - Weapon Familiarization

This includes skills like proper grip, sighting, loading and reloading, stances, selecting a weapon, and more. It also includes overlooked skills like drawing the weapon, dropping the safety, moving (walking, rolling, etc.) while drawing, aiming, and avoiding incoming fire.

2. Target-Hitting Skills - Shooting

This should seem fairly self-explanatory but, to be sure that I've covered my bases, this area also includes not only target shooting, but also skills like:

Shooting under pressure
Drawing and shooting
Off-hand shooting, and...

Firing from positions other than standard standing stances.

3. Disarming Skills - Taking the Attacker's Weapon

One of my teachers once told me that, you don't truly understand how to use a weapon until you know how to defend against it. This is true whether we're talking about a knife, martial arts long staff, club, or as in this case...a handgun.

Regardless of whether you're carrying a weapon of your own or not, it's quite possible that you could find yourself looking down the open-end of a barrel. Knowing how to avoid being shot while negotiating with your assailant or effectively taking his weapon away from him, is a critical skill to know.

And, contrary to popular belief, disarming an attacker is 95% psychology and only about 5% physical technique. Know "when" to make your move is often more important than "how" you do it.

And finally, the last pillar of mastery is...

4. Retention Skills - Holding On To Your Own Weapon

Most people, many experts included, are under the impression that, once you pull your weapon, the attacker is going to do whatever you say. And, while this seems logical, whoever said that people under pressure acted logically?

The truth of the matter is, you have no idea what he's thinking or what he might do when faced with the prospect of:

    Being shot
    Going (or going "back") to jail, or...
    Loosing

So, having the ability to hold onto your weapon should he (or anyone else who might try to help him) try to take your weapon from you is very important.

As you can see, when we're talking about weapons training for self-defense, we really have our work cut our for us. So, you have the choice of resting on theory and so-called "common-sense" or you can see that there is more to defending yourself with a firearm than simply being able to make a loud noise and have a hole appear in something.

To truly be able to handle a dangerous, life-threatening situation where a handgun is involved, you need to understand and develop the skills from the 4 pillars of mastery. That way, you wont have placed all your eggs in one basket. You will have insured that you can handle any type of situation that might arise.

My personal choices for survival-type weapons are as follows:

Handgun(s)

22 caliber long-rifle revolver or semi-automatic pistol. In truth if you're new to using a handgun I would suggest that you chose a revolver over a semi-automatic as it offers less complications in operations, is easier to reload and, though it holds fewer bullets, is as effective as a semi-automatic pistol.

The reason I chose 22 caliber is because first of all the cost for ammunition is far less than other calibers. For a box of 500 rounds you should, at today's current costs, be spending around forty dollars. Less than 500 rounds is okay but in reality you should have on hand all of the ammunition you can stockpile as you never know how long an emergent situation will or could last. No sense in having to hunt for food and have the added stress of not having enough ammunition to be able to do so effectively without having to worry about missing and wasting a bullet.

My choice for self-defense (although a 22 caliber will do the job of stopping aggressive actions) would be the 9mm. This is a common caliber and is used by the military in the U.S. Because it is so common you should be able to find it in most any big-box store like Wal-mart etc. If not you can find it online or at most sporting goods stores like Bass Pro etc. The cost is slightly higher than 22 caliber but you'll need less rounds to get the job done effectively.

Rifles:

Again my choice would have to be a 22 caliber. Prices for these fine rifles range from $150.00 on up depending on what fancy extras you want on them. Realistically you don't need anything but ammunition, good sights and the willingness to practice and you'll do just fine. Most small game is

able to be downed with the 22 caliber so you'll be able to hunt for the food you might need to feed your family should the need arise. In my opinion there is no such thing as poaching (hunting without a license) in the case of an emergency. I'd rather feed my family than starve, wouldn't you?

Long rang rifles for self defense vary greatly but in my opinion the 223 is a good choice. It shoots flat, fast and accurately. When someone hears the zing of a bullet passing near them they will stop and give pause to approaching you I'm sure. Practice with your weapon to become proficient and the 223 caliber will do a fine job for you in a survival situation.

Shotguns:

Most people would suggest that the 12 gauge shotgun should be your weapon of choice. I however differ with that. My choice would be the 20 gauge. It is just as effective as a defensive weapon and the recoil when shooting it is much less.

Cross Bow:

Earlier on I wrote about the bow and arrow. This too is a good choice but for a more effective way of using one I would suggest the cross bow. It shoots like a gun and is accurate, quiet and will take care of most wild game (or intruders) that you might have to put in your sites.

Use Open-Pollinated, Non-Hybrid Vegetable Seeds For Your Survival Garden.

Self perpetuating food sources should be a part of your everyday life. Any gardener will tell you that the taste of food you raise in your garden is far superior to hybridize store vegetables. In our opinion, there is no comparison to vegetables that are grown from seed. Beyond flavor, the nutritional value of your garden raised produce is also degrees beyond store produce. The ability to increase your health benefits is immeasurable.

But there is another benefit to growing your own vegetables: self-sustainability. A home-grown vegetable garden is the best vitamin and mineral source for your family, and it is your best hope for long-term survival in the event of a major national or global catastrophe.

As you know, 21st century farming relies on fuel and gas. In the event of a catastrophe or food famine (whether it be environmental, economic, or a natural disaster), it is likely that travel on interstate highways and major transportation routes (air, land, or sea) would be haulted. The large combines and tractors on the major food producing farms would likely be unable to operate and would just sit idle.

Did you know that the average grocery store can only store enough food to sustain a community for 2 or 3 days? In contrast, a simple 20x20 vegetable plot can yield over 600 pounds of produce - that's enough to feed a family of five for over a year. That's approximately $1500 worth of food. It's also a very small investment (around $100) that is worth it if you want to protect yourself in a state of emergency.

For survival purposes, there are other things to remember. A basic garden hoe and an almanac are also important items to store along with your non-hybrid / heirloom vegetable seeds and emergency preparedness supplies. It is unlikely that you would be able to go and purchase these items at a store during a crisis, so having the items on hand is essential.

Open-pollinated, non-hybrid seeds are the only choice for self-sustaining vegetable gardens because they are the only type of seed that can be gathered at harvest time and saved for the following year's planting cycle. As you grow and store your food, you can also store your vegetable seeds, making your small investment even more cost-effective. In addition, using seeds that will reproduce themselves for sustainability will ensure that seeds do not become extinct. Think about it: If the world encountered a major crisis and the viability of vegetable seeds was threatened, what would we do for food?

Near the North pole in Svalbard, Norway, food scientists are preparing for that possibility by collecting and storing thousands of non-hybrid, heirloom vegetable seeds. The vault contains three cold chambers that can hold a total of 4.5 million seed samples that would safeguard crops in the event of a catastrophe. The vault sits above sea level to ensure it isn't destroyed by rising waters. It's resistant to nuclear attacks and the permafrost will keep the seeds fresh even if the system's freezer system fails.

If food scientists and countries around the world are concerned about having enough seed for the future, why shouldn't each of us prepare in a similar way? We believe that preparing for a crisis by having enough seeds to feed our families is the right answer. It isn't necessary for us to store millions of seeds - but a small vegetable plot that can yield plenty of food is a good start.

Final Thoughts

I have covered a lot of material in this book and I hope that you have come to the conclusion that survival isn't simply about hopping in your bug-out-vehicle and heading out of town. Indeed it is far more than that. Without proper planning, training and the will to survive you're going to run into problems you never imagined and will be hard pressed to overcome.

Training and preparation is critical. Without it you'll wonder around without direction or purpose and that is the worst case scenario you want to find yourself in.

I encourage you to take the time to prepare now before circumstances, weather related or man-made, present themselves and you find that you've not prepared enough to keep yourself, your family or others around you safe and secure.

Happy Trails. Stay safe and secure and with any luck I'll see you on the safe side of whatever befalls you in life.

"Survival is the celebration of choosing life over death. We know we're going to die. We all die. But survival is saying: perhaps not today. In that sense, survivors don't defeat death, they come to terms with it."

If you enjoyed reading and learning from this book I have another one that I wrote and published a while back. It deals specifically with prepping; who should and who should not be a prepper and why along with methods of prepping that could save your life.

Click this link and you'll be taken directly to Amazon. From there you can purchase my book with one simple click.

http://www.amazon.com/gp/product/B00GTVTNSY